Anyone Can Draw

Drawing is fun – but isn't it disappointing when the shapes and lines on your paper simply don't look like the exciting pictures in your head? Well, here is a practical guide to the basic rules of drawing (with lots of illustrations to copy or trace) which will help you to improve your skills. Many different subjects are covered, including cartoons. (Find out how to draw 'running' cartoons, like the one that runs through this book, in Chapter 8.)

THIS ARMADA BOOK BELONGS TO:

James P. Talbot.

ALBERT MURFY & SARA SILCOCK

Anyone Can Draw

Introduced by TONY HART

An Armada Original

Anyone Can Draw was first published in the
U.K. in 1981 in Armada by
Fontana Paperbacks,
14 St. James's Place, London SW1A 1PS

© Text and illustrations 1981
by Victorama Ltd.

Made and printed by The Anchor Press,
Tiptree, Essex

CHAPTER 1

The Rules to Start With

When you think about it, a drawing is only a few marks on a surface, and it is only the way the marks are laid out that suggests they are not just a collection of accidental smudges, but are describing something.

With the help of a very few marks and changes of direction you get someone to 'read' a picture, by prompting their imagination to fill in all the missing details, and ignore all the inaccuracies and mistakes you have made.

Also, by the way you have drawn the lines, you can show whether something is hard or soft.

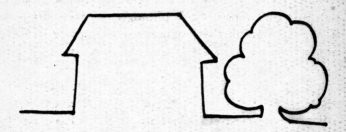

The house has hard lines and sharp corners, and, although the lines aren't perfectly straight, you do get the idea that the building is rigid. Compare that to the tree, which looks much softer.

Suppose that the same drawing was slightly different:

Your imagination won't accept that quite as readily, will it?

There must be very few people – even those who say, "I couldn't draw if you paid me a million pounds!" – who can't join a few lines together to produce something that can be read as a drawing. What they mean when they say that they can't draw is that they can't do a picture which looks like a photograph. Well, if they want a photograph, they ought to use a camera!

When you take a photograph, the film responds to the varying amounts of light coming in through the lens of the camera, but when you do a drawing, you not only respond to the light you see, you also choose which bits of what you are looking at you wish to draw.

You can exaggerate or play things down – or can even introduce details that are completely made-up. It's up to you.

In other words, a drawing is what you make it, and – whether it's good or bad – no-one can say it's *wrong*. You are a human camera.

The only problem you'll find is that you can never draw exactly what you want to. But don't worry, this is a problem that everyone has, even the greatest artist ever. All anyone can do if they really want to get closer to that brilliant picture in their mind's eye is to find a method on which to 'build' their drawing so that it won't collapse under the weight of a few mistakes.

Before you start to draw, here are a few simple guidelines to help you:

1. Perhaps the most obvious (whether you are drawing in or out of doors) is make sure you are comfortable before you start. If you are uncomfortable it will show in your drawing.

2. Use a drawing board or at least some thick cardboard to rest your paper on and get some bulldog clips or proper drawingboard clips to stop the paper from sliding about.

Indoors, use a table top (with newspaper or other padding underneath if it is your best polished table) and put some cushions on your chair if necessary so that you get a good over-all view of your drawing and can move your arms freely.

3. Make sure you have a good light when you draw because it makes your eyes very tired if you have to peer into the shade to see what you're doing. Indoors, some sort of table lamp is best, to the left of your drawing if you are right-handed and to the right if you are left-handed. This will save the annoyance of having the line you have just drawn disappearing into the shadow of your hand.

4. Experiment, if you like, with different drawing instruments. They all have their own particular qualities, although the tried and tested pencil is probably the best and easiest to use for a straight-forward drawing. Pencils come in many different grades, from 10H, which is extremely hard and almost invisible, and only used in very specialist jobs, to 10B, which is very soft and very black, and

also very smudgy. For everyday use an HB or B (the middle of the range) are about the best to use, but try a 2B or 3B for a large or more energetic picture. The great advantage about these pencils, apart from the fact that you can rub out bad mistakes easily, is that you can draw faint or bold black lines.

Other instruments to try:

Felt Pens and Fibre Pens: The felt pen comes in many thicknesses and colours, but it is usually more used when colouring a picture or for designing patterns. The fibre-point pen can produce much thinner and stronger lines, and doesn't wear out quite as quickly.

Charcoal and Chalk: There is charcoal and chalk for larger drawings, and both can be messy and smudgy, and not very good for drawing details. To avoid losing a chalk or charcoal (or even a pencil) drawing in a cloud of smudges once you have finished it, you can use an aerosol spray fixative, which produces an invisible coat all over the drawing. These sprays can be bought from any artshop, but be careful that you spray it in a well-ventilated room, or better still, outdoors.

Drawing Pen: A drawing pen – or 'dip pen' – has been used for a long time, and with Indian ink can help produce strong drawings, although you can also use it to draw tiny details. Its great advantage is that with the same blackness you can draw nice thick lines by pressing hard, and wispy thin lines by just touching the paper. Of course, there is no need to use only black ink, as you can buy many bright colours of waterproof

15

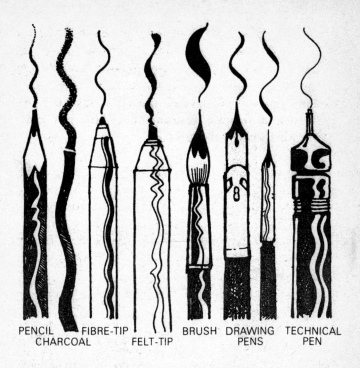

PENCIL FIBRE-TIP BRUSH DRAWING TECHNICAL
CHARCOAL FELT-TIP PENS PEN

ink, which are also useful for colouring in drawings using a brush and water.

The Technical Pen: Finally, and most expensively, there is the technical pen – so called because it was designed to be used by designers and architects, who need to do very accurate and complicated drawings, using rulers and compasses. You may have discovered that if you use a drawing pen and a ruler to draw a straight line, you can be pretty sure that most of the ink will find its way off the pen and under the ruler, producing an irritating splodgy mess. There is no such problem with a technical pen. They are made to draw in various thicknesses, and each one will only draw one thickness or 'weight' of line. If you try pressing the nib on to the paper as you would a drawing pen, instead of a thicker line you will have a broken pen. Also, because it is such a delicate instrument, it will not draw satisfactorily on rough paper.

A paintbrush, of course, can be used for drawing too, and, with practice, can produce very attractive results, but, for ordinary every-day use, stick to the pencil!

Remember that whatever instrument you use, treat it with care. A pencil can easily be ruined if you play the drums with it. Felt and fibre-tip pens will dry out if you leave the tops off. Brushes will go bald if you let paint or ink dry in them, or if you leave them standing in water. And of course, pens that are treated like darts don't last very long.

Pads of cartridge paper are a very convenient way of buying and using paper, but are much more expensive than buying loose sheets of the same quality, which you can buy at any reasonable artshop.

So why not just have a small sketch pad to carry about with you wherever you go, and use the larger looser sheets for drawing expeditions and for using at home on your drawing board or table.

CHAPTER 2

Drawing People

As with all solid objects, people are made up of a collection of very simple shapes, and it is only the details that are stuck on top that tend to confuse us into thinking that they are more complicated.

So if we use these simple shapes as the structure and then build on top we can be more confident that if there are any mistakes they won't ruin the whole picture. It will also be easier to spot any mistakes.

The common way to start a drawing of, say, a face, is to hop from one feature to another, joining them up like pieces of a jigsaw puzzle, and hoping that each bit of the drawing is exactly the right size and in exactly the right place. In other words, that it is all 'in proportion'.

But if the picture is started by looking at all the big shapes, starting with the biggest, then we'll know that the basic structure is all right.

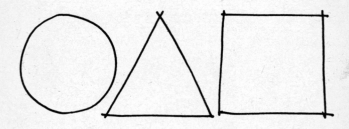

These are the basic shapes that can be used in every drawing, and, by combining them, using bits of them or slightly distorting them, they are a perfect basis for a picture.

The Head

The first decision to be made after drawing a circle is what is the distinctive shape of the head within the circle. For example, is it:

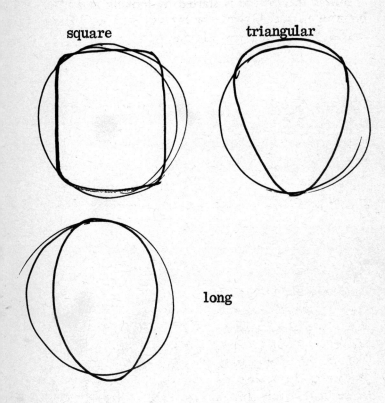

square

triangular

long

Don't be distracted by details. Just keep your eye on the overall shape.

Once you have decided and drawn the shape, stage two is to decide where the features are in the shape. That is, where the eyes, ears, nose, mouth and hair are. Think of your circle as a ball, and divide the ball into lines where you think the various features are positioned.

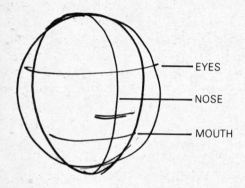

Then look at each feature and decide which of the basic shapes they most look like.

Are the eyes, for instance, like everyone imagines eyes, or are they more square? Or triangular?

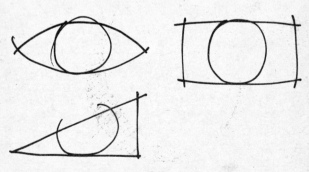

Take nothing for granted, and look at everything carefully. Don't draw what you think you know. Draw what you see.

Continue adding to the drawing, all the time looking for the shapes, and if you are getting lost in all the guidelines, tidy them up with a rubber. If they don't bother you, leave them. They will help you to see how you've 'built' a drawing, when you've finished it.

When you feel that you've drawn everything in the right place and in the right proportion (you can check this more easily if you turn the drawing upside down or hold it to a mirror to see if it all holds together) use light and shade to make everything look more solid.

Again, think simply – don't try to 'capture' every little fold and wrinkle.

Firstly, decide where the light is coming from. Perhaps draw a quick sketch in the corner of the paper to remind you. Then draw in the large areas of shade, thinking of the shapes.

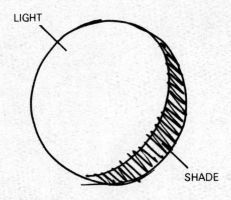

LIGHT

SHADE

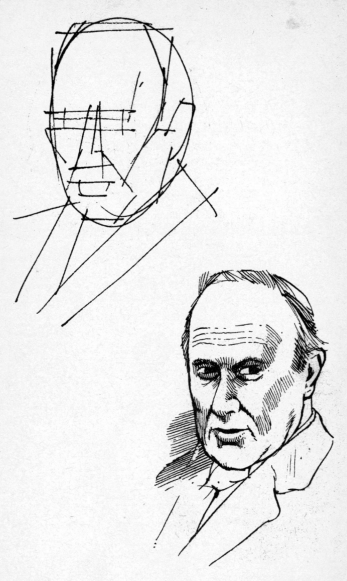

24

25

Although the face is the most recognisable part of a person, it will mean much more if it is attached to a body, rather than floating around the paper like a planet in outer space.

So whether you are getting someone to sit for you, or are drawing a self-portrait with a mirror, sketch in simply the position of everything that you want to include. This will save the problem that often happens when someone is so keen to get on with the picture that they start in the middle of the paper with the most interesting bit, and find that as they reach the bottom of the page they have to start squashing everything up to fit it in.

A few simple lines are all you need. This is called 'composing' the picture. Don't be distracted by any folds or creases in the clothes.

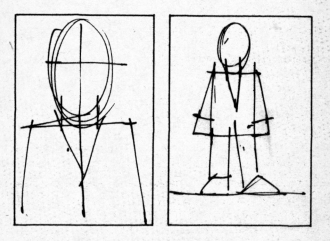

26

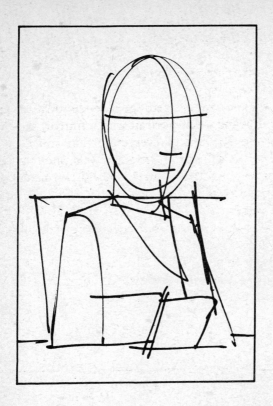

Once you are used to composing a picture before you start, and you want to do a special drawing (a portrait to give to someone, perhaps) rather than a study, think about a more interesting layout for the drawing. Imagine that the edges of your paper are the frame, and that what you are going to draw are just 'abstract' shapes or patterns.

Look at what is in the background that would make the picture more interesting. Then imagine your subject as a shape in different parts of the frame.

It is usually the case that something plonked right in the middle of the picture is much less exciting to the eye of the viewer than if it were thoughtfully placed. Also, still thinking of everything as abstract shapes – as if they were cut out of different coloured papers – the greater difference there is between the size of shapes, the more eye-catching and therefore more exciting the picture is, even before your admiring viewer has looked properly at the drawing.

This is called 'contrast' and can be used in several different ways to good effect: big and small, black and white, fat and thin, long and short.

31

CHAPTER 3

Drawing Animals

Whatever you like drawing, the more you draw the more you improve. But, in contrast to the subject of the previous chapter, where even if everyone has gone to a football match, or no-one will sit still for you, you can always sit in front of a mirror and draw what you see, animals are far less helpful.

Even the cat that has been sprawling in front of the fire with only a twitch will get up and have a wash when you start to draw it. Although you know that the cat moved on purpose, you must smile graciously and try to draw it anyway.

If, however, there are no animals around, then turn to photographs, or even other people's drawings (as long as they are good drawings – if they are not, look at them and decide why you think they fail).

On the face of it, animals would seem much more difficult to draw than people. This partly because they haven't got any obvious expressions, but mainly because most of them are covered in fluff, scales, fur or feathers. How can you draw something that's hidden in FLUFF?!!

Well, simply by follow-
ing the same principle
as with drawing
people. Look for
all the basic
shapes, and
don't get lost
in all the
fluff.

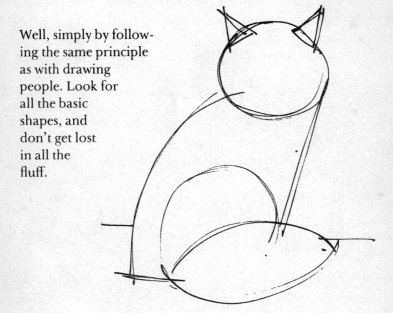

Map out all the basic shapes lightly in pencil, forget-ting for the moment that you are drawing fluff. Then look for the obvious features – the eyes, nose, mouth etc., and sketch in their positions lightly, using guidelines.

Look carefully at the shapes you have created and make sure they are all in proportion to one another, then carefully add more details.

Obviously, with a subject like a fluffy cat, you can't hope to draw all the fluff, however sharp your pencil and steady your hand – especially if it's a white cat. It would end up looking more like a Brillo pad. Instead, you draw an impression of the fluff, so that you give a feeling of it, which someone else looking at the

drawing will understand
and 'read'.

Look at the way different areas of fluff are moving
and the shapes they are making, and draw the areas.
Are they spiky? Or soft waves? Ask yourself questions
as you look. A lot will depend on the way you draw the
lines.

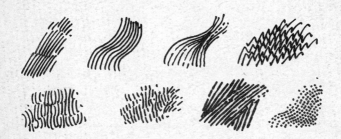

Practice drawing different sorts of lines to give varying feelings or 'textures'.

Make sure that these 'shorthand' areas fit in with the overall shapes that you drew originally. Of course, with short-haired or hairless animals, there isn't the same problem, although keep in mind the same thoughts about the texture you are drawing.

For the final stage of the drawing introduce light and shade, as with the previous chapter. Try not to get confused between dark colours (patches, dark fur, etc.) and shadows.

It is the shading that gives the picture the feeling that it is solid, so concentrate on this first, wherever possible using shading lines that follow the direction of the fur or hair, or the shape of the body.

Then, for any patches, stripes or colouring, draw over the top in a darker line, again following the direction of any fur, or the shape of the body.

Don't shade in more than is necessary. It's easily possible to ruin a drawing by putting in too many 'finishing touches'.

On the following pages there are drawings of lots of different animals which show how all sorts of textures and effects can be achieved.

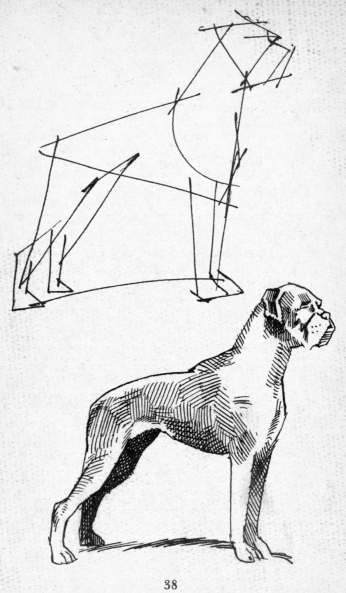

38

40

41

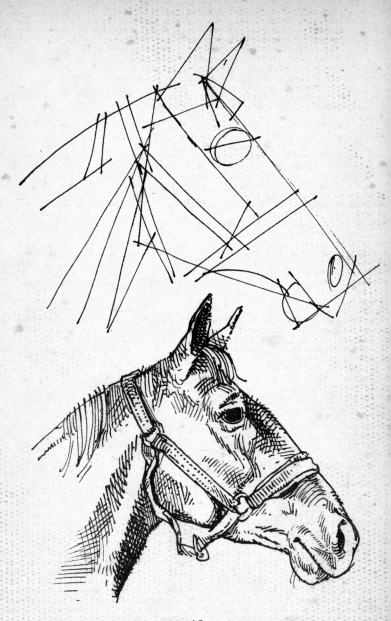

44

45

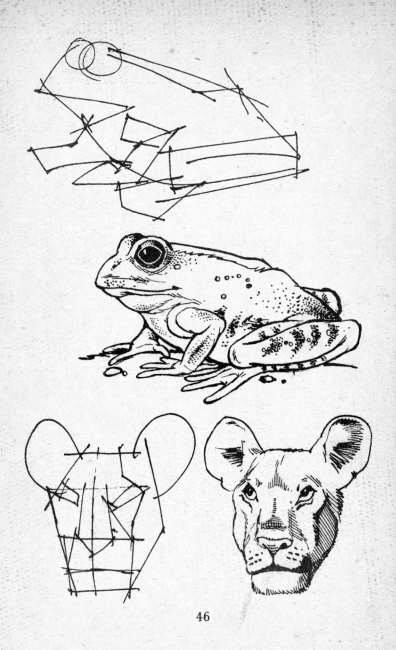

46

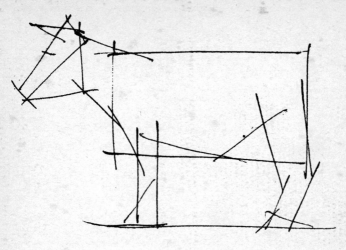

47

CHAPTER 4

Drawing Everyday Objects

Whatever you are drawing in what is traditionally known as 'still-life', everything has its own set of basic shapes, as do people and animals.

Whether you are drawing something as simple as an apple, or as complicated as a car, try to break the drawing down in exactly the same way.

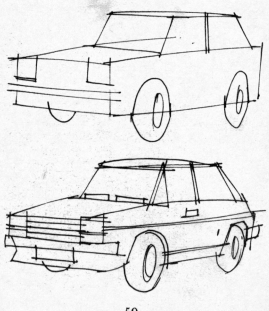

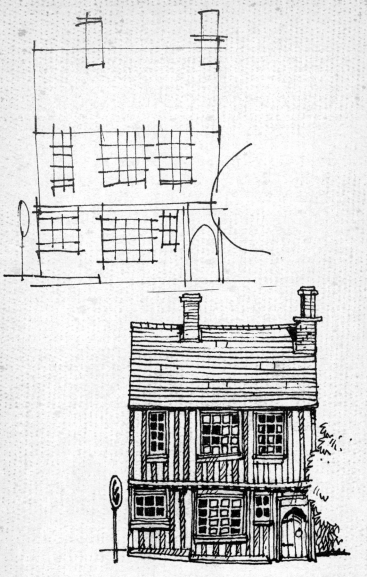

Take, for instance, a pot-plant. You might find that the flowers are the most interesting part of the plant, but don't just concentrate on a beautiful drawing of one flower, and then try to join the rest of the plant to it. The chances are that it won't fit on to the paper. Look at the overall shape of the plant, including the pot. Ask yourself if it's long, oval, square, triangular or a simple combination of shapes. Of course, this doesn't mean that every leaf-tip has to fit within your shape, as long as you have got the overall description.

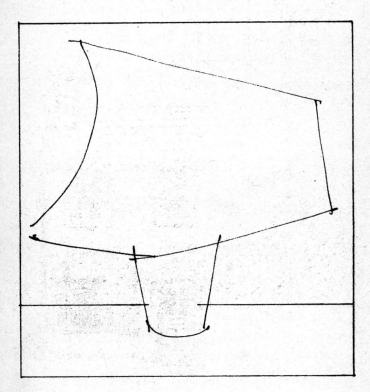

Next, sketch in the area taken by the pot (which gives your subject its base) followed by the general direction of the stem or stems.

Do this by the same method. Sketch in the leaf area, and the route of the leaf stalk through the middle of the leaf and on to the stem of the plant. Within the overall shape of the flower, work out the shapes of the petals. Only after you are satisfied that everything is in proportion should you start drawing the details that give the plant its particular character.

You can now map in the clusters of leaves and flowers, and then draw in the shapes of the individual leaves.

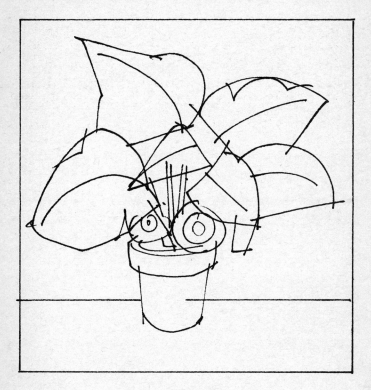

Lightly work in the vein system on the leaves where you can see them, and gradually 'tighten up' the drawing. That is, draw careful, confident lines when you are sure you know where they go, helped by your basic sketch.

If you try a drawing like this, why not take it a little further by using a drawing pen and some

waterproof indian ink to draw in the delicate lines of
the plant (or whatever subject you decide to draw),
then rub out all the pencil lines with a good quality
rubber to leave the pure black pen lines.

Then, with watercolours or coloured inks and a
brush, colour in the drawing, matching the colours
that you can see as closely as you can.

Perhaps finish the drawing by brushing in a light
wash over the background, though not necessarilly
painting up to the pen lines.

Of course, the great advantage with still objects is that they don't get fed-up with sitting still, so by drawing anything and everything around you you will find that all your drawings – of people, animals and still objects – will get much better.

You will automatically get much better at controlling your pencil, and at looking at what you are drawing.

As these objects won't complain, you can spend much more time working on a drawing, so why not try out various compositions and arrangements on your paper?

CHAPTER 5

Drawing Landscapes

Drawing landscapes probably calls for more thought-ful composition than the previous subjects because, although you can use the same method of working out the drawing as before (using simple lines) there are also other things to think about.

The main point is to remember that every picture needs a centre of attention – a 'focal point'. This doesn't mean that your drawing must have something strange or fascinating in it somewhere, and you don't have to spend more time drawing it than anything else. The picture simply needs something to 'hold it down' rather like a paperweight holds down a piece of paper.

Take the most ridiculously simple picture ... a desert scene, and how BORING!

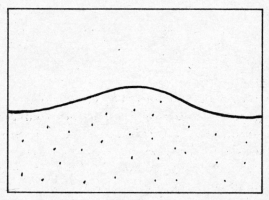

But by slipping in one tiny item, a palm tree, you have made the picture much more interesting. It gives you some idea of scale, apart from helping you to understand what you are looking at.

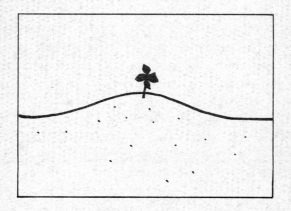

Of course, this is a silly drawing, but the idea behind it is exactly the same in whatever landscape you draw, however detailed. If you are using a landscape as a background to some particular subject – say, a gate or a bridge, then of course you don't have the same problem, because you already have the centre of interest.

Another equally important tip to remember to avoid boring your viewer is how to balance your picture. Back to the desert . . . with the tree stuck right in the middle of the picture with a nicely balanced horizon running right through the middle of the page there is a very tidy, very neat picture – but so uninteresting!

If the horizon was moved away from the middle of the page, either up or down, and if the dunes and the tree were moved to the sides, or at least off-centre, there is immediately a more interesting arrangement.

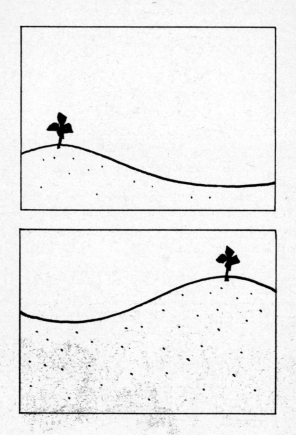

It grabs your attention, as if it were moving, instead of sitting there quietly, not bothering anybody, like the previous example.

So, whenever you start a drawing, if you can remember to make sure that you don't sit everything interesting right in the middle, or have it all beautifully balanced, then you won't have people falling asleep in front of your finished picture.

Another way of keeping someone's attention is to use the fact that your drawing is something like the view through a window, with the edge of the paper acting as a window-frame.

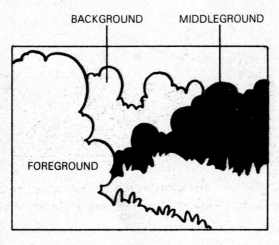

BACKGROUND   MIDDLEGROUND

FOREGROUND

To help draw their eye through the window frame (in other words, to make the drawing feel real), make sure you have something in the foreground to 'help them through'. It doesn't have to be important or detailed, or in the way.

For example, if you put part of a tree to the side of your drawing, it will give you the feeling that you are standing under the tree, admiring the view in front of you – especially if you make it a dark shape, as if you were in the shade, contrasting with the landscape beyond.

Look for something particular to use as a step when you start drawing. It could be part of a fence, a

signpost, an old piece of farm machinery, or even a clump of grass. By trying different objects in different ways you will find that you can alter the feeling of scale and distance in a picture.

CHAPTER 6

Drawing From Your Imagination

Drawing from your imagination may sound easier than drawing what you see in front of you, and in a way it is, because you are inventing the subject. But you can really only invent from what you know – from what you have seen. Your imagination needs feeding just as an engine needs fuel. The more you supply your imagination with food, the better and more imaginative it will be. It thrives on observation, and of course the best way to observe things is to draw them.

By making your hand follow what your eye is looking at somehow seems to record it inside your brain, as if you had an imaginary notebook between your ears.

In case you are not convinced, try a simple exercise. Without sneaking another look, do a drawing from your memory of something you see every day – perhaps your bike, or the television – something you know well.

Draw all the details you can remember, and only when you have finished take the drawing and compare it with the real thing. You'll be amazed at how wrong you were, at what you forgot and at what you invented or put in the wrong place.

This doesn't mean that whenever you want to do a drawing from your imagination you have to spend hours studying and drawing anything that might be of use to you. It's just that the more you draw – people, animals, objects, buildings or landscapes, the keener your imagination will be.

Suppose that you wanted to do a science-fiction scene, with Earthmen exploring a strange planet. The more you had noticed about how people move and how their clothes fold and crease, how everyday plants grow and differ and how various real-life animals are built, the more your imagination has to work on.

67

This is very similar to the way that designers of science-fiction films take pieces of everyday objects – hair-dryers, salt-cellars, ping-pong balls and so on, and, with imagination and a lick of paint, turn them into those weird but realistic spacecraft that you see hurtling through the galaxies.

Of course, drawing from your imagination doesn't necessarily mean science-fiction scenes. You can draw anything from the most ordinary every-day subjects to the most fantastic images your brain can invent. It all depends on what interests you, or what mood you are in.

Try illustrating a scene from a book you have read, or a story you have been told, using the guidelines that appear in other chapters for composition, contrast and so on. If you get stuck, and can't remember what a particular object looks like (your imagination can't think of everything!) then look for something to help you – some kind of reference.

A pictorial encylopaedia is an extremely useful source of supply, as are any magazines, if you can't find an example of the real thing. You will find that the occasional 'top-up' of information will give your drawing a more convincing feeling, even if you bend and distort the result of your reference almost beyond recognition.

If you find that your imagination gets really inspired, you could try writing your own stories and then illustrating them, or writing a story around your drawing.

Whatever the subject of your drawing, try to keep

the mood of your picture in mind all the time. For instance, if you are drawing a very peaceful scene, where everything is calm and quiet, draw it in a 'peaceful' way, with calm, gentle lines and strokes. Or if your drawing is to be a wild, violent subject, make the lines and shapes bold and heavy. Likewise, if it is to be a happy picture, think happy. Or sad, think sad.

If you can think yourself into the right frame of mind, using your imagination, you will have no problem, and your picture should take on a life of its own. It might even add to the quality of the result if you listened to 'mood' music (music that reflects the feeling you are trying to suggest in your picture) while you are drawing.

Look at drawings in books and magazines to see how they manage (or fail) to suggest imagined situations. And don't be afraid to copy any drawing or part of a drawing that impresses you, because this will help you to discover how a particular technique is achieved. This is rather like taking a machine apart to see how it works.

CHAPTER 7

Drawing For Cheats

If you really can't get anywhere with the previous chapters, there are only two choices left to you – give up or cheat. Well, don't give up yet, because cheating isn't as bad as it sounds.

It's annoying for anyone if their picture doesn't turn out well, so what you need are some short cuts to producing an attractive and interesting picture.

Tracing is a very useful method. Take a photograph – not a valuable original (because a hard pencil traced over it will make ugly grooves in the print) but perhaps a picture from a magazine.

Tab a sheet of tracing paper over it with two hinges of sticky tape and trace round all the shapes in the photo as carefully and accurately as you can with a hard sharp pencil (an H or 2H).

Then with a softer pencil (a 2B or 3B), rub over the back of the tracing under all the lines you have traced, then smudge it all smoothly with a tissue or cotton wool.

Tab the tracing paper on to a good clean piece of

cartridge paper (or white board if you have any) and draw over the traced lines with the hard pencil, so that they print down on to the paper.

Then with a pen, draw over the lines on the paper, rub out the pencil marks, and, with the photograph in front of you, paint in all the dark shapes with Indian ink.

The result should be an attractive and recognisable picture.

You could also try colouring in the shapes you have drawn or drawing it on coloured paper, to turn it into a cross between an exciting pattern and a recognisable drawing.

If you find that your pencil just wanders off on its own as soon as it touches the paper, and it won't even trace the shapes you want it to ... never fear! Give it something to lean on. Use anything – matchboxes, rulers, coins, the bottoms of bottles, etc., for it to cling to so it won't get lost. With a pencil, or perhaps a thin felt pen, use whatever you can find that helps you draw the roughly-right lines. They will produce some really attractive results. Don't try to be too accurate with what you draw, and don't try to alter or clean up any lines.

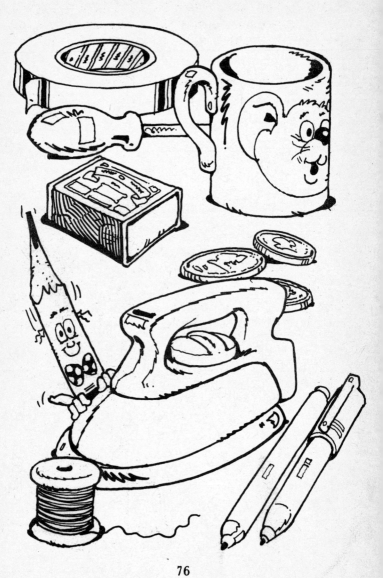

Follow the basic guidelines for drawing, that is, draw the big shapes first, and then slowly add more detail, so that you don't find that you've run off the edge of the paper.

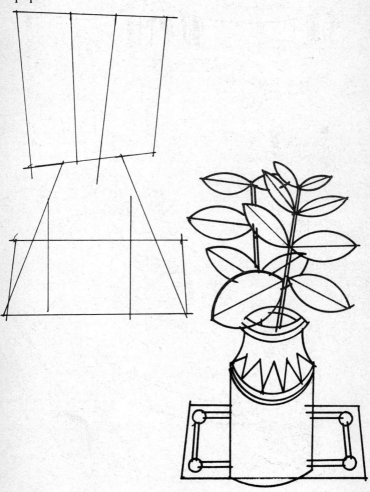

You'll be surprised at the freshness of your picture, but, to brighten it further, try using coloured paper, or colouring in with simple colours.

Try a simple drawing first, and as you gain confidence have a go at a more complicated subject, but don't stop to think whether you are being accurate, or even if the drawing is recognisable. Finally, colour in the shapes that you have created, thinking more of their exciting effect than how close they are to the real thing.

CHAPTER 8

Drawing Cartoons

A good cartoon drawing comes from a good drawing. All that happens to turn it into a cartoon is that everything is made simpler, and the obvious main features are exaggerated – drawn larger.

It is with cartooning that the method of using simple shapes becomes even more important, because these simple shapes are often the only things that hold a cartoon drawing together. After all, the word 'cartoon' originally meant a drawing that was done in preparation for a painting. It was not supposed to be funny.

Remember all the time to use simple shapes.

There are many standard 'codes' to show expression. Here are a few. Try drawing some of your own as simply as you can.

You can use these in all your cartoons, whether they are of humans, or animals – or even more unusual things . . .

Start by drawing a simple pattern that will hardly change, whatever expression you give it.

These are the eyes and nose, then depending where you put the eyebrows, eyelids, pupils and mouth, you can produce a wide range of expressions.

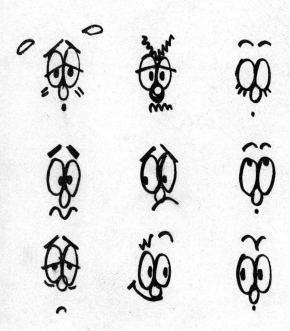

To make your experiments easier, and to help you work out your final drawings, try using 'layout' or bank paper, which can be bought at artshops that supply materials to design studios. This paper is thin and easier (and cheaper) to draw on than tracing paper, and lets you work out your drawing on one sheet, with all its mistakes and changes of mind. Then with another sheet that you can see through over the top, you can draw your final cartoon choosing only the right lines.

Good references are very useful – that is, photographs, and serious drawings of the subject you wish to draw. From these you can understand what gives your subject its special appearance.

Now here is the method in action, starting with the very first stage.

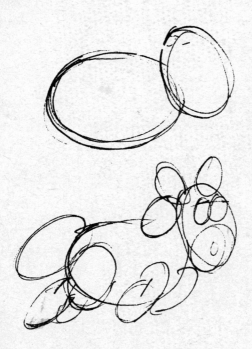

(There are lots of special codes that cartoonists use to show their subjects in action, and these are best discovered by looking at the finished drawings and perhaps jotting them down in a special notebook.)

Try making your own cartoons. Choose a character – any sort of recognisable person or animal, although don't pick one that would be too complicated to draw quickly – and imagine him/her in funny situations. And remember: whatever you draw for the background, keep it as simple as you can, or it will stand out too much.

You can also try producing some comic strips. Invent a few characters that amuse you, and that you can tell stories about, then imagine them in different situations. Perhaps, to get used to the idea, base the characters on you and your friends, and draw them doing what you have been doing.

You could start a comic diary.

Don't be too ambitious at first. Start with three or four boxes. The size depends on you, but if you make them too big they will be hard to fill up, and if they are too small, they will be difficult to draw in.

About 10 cm. square should be a comfortable size, although of course you don't have to make them square.

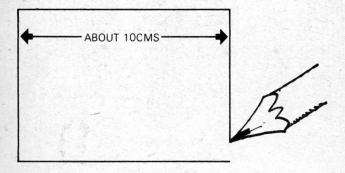

ABOUT 10CMS

Keep the comic strip very simple and to the point, so that your joke or story isn't lost in all the complicated detail.

Your drawing can be made to look more lively and interesting if you draw in the boxes with a ruler, and do the cartoons freehand.

Once you have mastered the simple comic strip be more adventurous and try telling stories.

Backgrounds can often be suggested very easily by using a simple line, which doesn't get in the way of your subject.

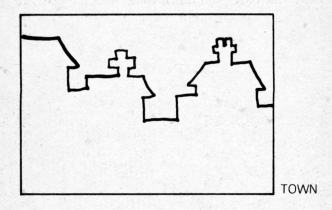

TOWN

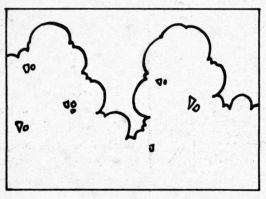

COUNTRY

Moving cartoons may sound complicated and difficult, but in fact you can draw very effective ones easily – just like the one running through this book. By putting a series of small drawings in the top right-hand corner of a spare notebook, one on each page, you can flick over the pages and watch your cartoon move. All you need to work out are two simple movements, then trace them down alternately in the same position on each page.

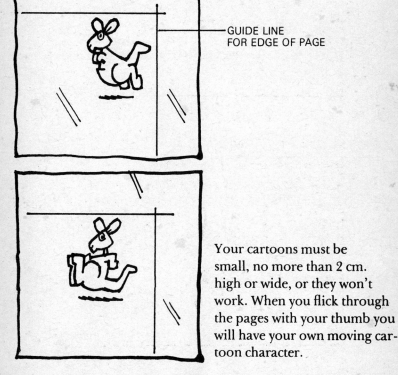

TRACING PAPER

GUIDE LINE
FOR EDGE OF PAGE

Your cartoons must be small, no more than 2 cm. high or wide, or they won't work. When you flick through the pages with your thumb you will have your own moving cartoon character.

CHAPTER 9

Six Points to Remember

1.   Whatever living being you wish to draw, it is useful to know how it is made up. That is, what the basic skeleton and muscles look like. The bone structure is especially useful because it will help you to work out which way the joints bend and how they can move.

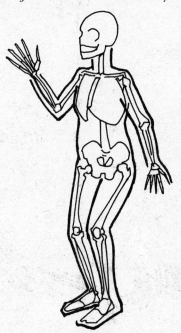

2. Draw as much as you can so that it becomes a habit. Make quick ('lightning') sketches of things you see around you. These will help you to see the basic

93

shapes in everything and how they look as they move, apart from improving your drawing ability.

3.   Don't give up hope on a drawing if it doesn't go quite right. Perhaps have a rest and come back to it refreshed. The more drawings you can rescue from disaster the more you will learn.

4. Ask for others' opinions on your pictures, but don't get upset if they don't like them.

5. Look at other people's drawings, and try to work out what is good or bad about them, and why you like or dislike them.

6. Have fun!